D1390189

leap THROUGH TIME

Transport

First published in 2004 by Orpheus Books Ltd, 2 Church Green,
Witney, Oxon OX28 4AW

Copyright © 2004 Orpheus Books Ltd

All rights reserved. No part of this book may be reproduced or utilized
in any form or by any means, electronic or mechanical, including
photocopying, recording or by any information storage and retrieval
system, without permission in writing from the publisher except by a
reviewer who may quote brief passages in a review.

Created and produced by Nicholas Harris, Claire Aston and
Emma Godfrey, Orpheus Books Ltd

Text Nicholas Harris

Illustrator Peter Dennis *(Linda Rogers Associates)*

Consultant Dr John Griffiths, Senior Curator, Science Museum,
London, England

ISBN 1 901323 81 1

Printed and bound in Malaysia

Transport

illustrated by

Peter David Scott

Orpheus

Contents

4

Introduction

Imagine you are somewhere in Europe, not far from the coast, thousands of years ago. Oxcarts rumble along dirt tracks. Out to sea, a small sailing ship cuts through the waves. As the years go by, roads and bridges are built. A small quay is constructed, allowing ships to moor in the harbour. Gradually, people are able to travel farther, faster and in greater comfort.

The story told in this book is like a journey. It is not a journey you can make by plane, car or ship. In fact, you don't have to go anywhere at all. You are about to travel through *time*. With each turn of the page, the date moves forward a few years or even centuries. Each new date—each stop on your journey—is like a chapter in the story. The first carts and carriages, early sailing ships, the building of canals and railways, the invention of steam engines and the first steam locomotives and steamships, the arrival of petrol-driven cars and the conquest of the skies by aircraft, the building of docks, an airport and a suspension bridge—all tell the story of transport.

Look out for the pair of lovers. They appear in all of the illustrations, although sometimes they are quite difficult to spot.

Use this thumb index to travel through time! Just find the page you want to see and flip it open. This way you can make a quick comparison between one scene and another, even though some show events that took place many years apart. A little black arrow on the page points to the time of the scene illustrated on that page.

About 3000 years ago ...

People travel along rough tracks in carts drawn by their animals. Oxen and mules pull heavy loads of hay or grain while horses are harnessed to faster vehicles. Some young men are practising their driving skills in war chariots, but they are in danger of colliding with slow-moving farm traffic!

Oxcart

Rowing boats

All road vehicles must cross the stream at a ford, a place where the water is shallow enough to wade across. Only those on foot can use the small wooden bridge. Some people travel downstream in circular rowing boats made from woven twigs and animal skins. Out at sea a wooden sailing boat cruises by.

Hillfort

Thatched roof

War chariots

Bridge

Ford

A thousand years later ...

The Romans have conquered these lands. Where once there stood a simple hillfort, the soldiers have built a stronger stone fortress. The old rough farm tracks have been replaced by proper paved roads. Chariots, ox wagons and legions of Roman soldiers all cross the river by a sturdy bridge.

Aqueduct

Inn

Clabularia
(ox wagon)

Ditch

Groma

Digging foundations
for road

The Romans have also built an aqueduct. Its stone arches support a canal which carries water across the valley.

ROMAN ROADS

The Romans built 85,000 kilometres of roads across their empire. Built as straight as possible, they allowed soldiers and messengers to make quick progress in all weathers. Surveyors used an instrument called a *groma* to mark out right angles. The roads were made of layers of sand and stone.

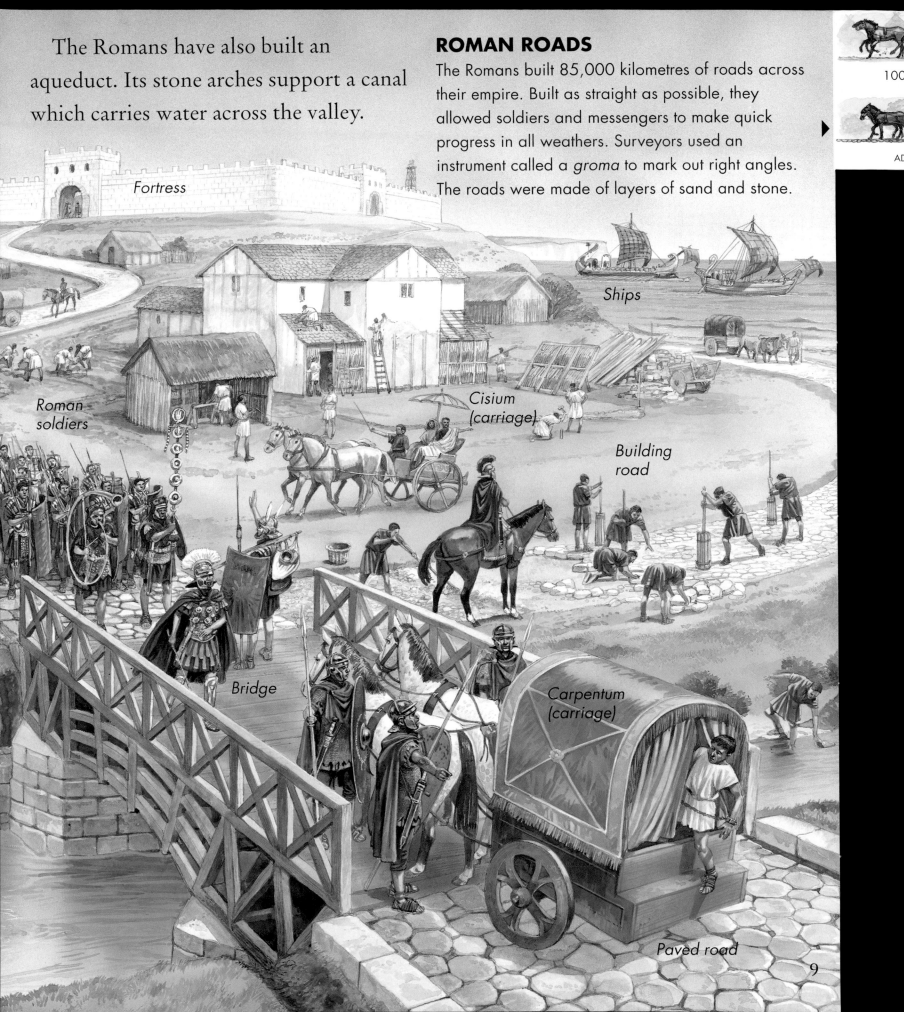

Fortress

Ships

Roman soldiers

Cisium (carriage)

Building road

Bridge

Carpentum (carriage)

Paved road

9

ships followed
design as Viking
. It was not until
t the ocean-
ee-masted
peared.

About 1300 years later ...

The Romans have long since gone. The aqueduct lies in ruins, but a magnificent castle stands in place of the fortress.

Down by the waterfront, a trading ship, called a cog, has just moored. This craft has a single square mast and a hull built with overlapping planks. There are "castles" at the stern and the bow.

Ruined aqueduct

Inn

Carriage

Monks

Stepping ashore is a visiting lady. She is greeted by the lord of the castle, together with knights, guards, musicians and servants.

A luxurious carriage awaits to carry the lord's guest back up to the castle. Onlookers gather as carts and horses are loaded up with the lady's possessions.

Castle

Old Roman road

Stern "castle"

Pilgrims

Knight

Lord

Lady

Quay

Cog

Bow "castle"

century,
asure ships,
ons, sailed to
e Americas,
d and silver.

About 400 years later ...

Terror strikes! Arab pirates from the northern coast of Africa, known as Barbary corsairs, suddenly appear. They have sailed hundreds of kilometres north in their sleek, fast galleys in search of slaves. Brandishing their curved *nimcha* swords and guns, they launch a surprise attack on the port's inhabitants.

Nobody is safe from the corsairs. Wealthy men and women travelling in their fine horse-drawn carriages or sedan chairs are seized and led towards the ship.

Inn

Carriage

Captives

While the corsairs ransack the harbour, a carriage has been stopped by a highwayman carrying a pistol. He demands money from the people inside.

Castle

Quay

Highwayman

Sedan chair

Chebek (corsair galley)

13

About 125 years later ...

The port has become much busier. While sailing ships—and some small steam ships—load up with cargo, carriages of all kinds stream along the quayside road.

One of the carriages has no horses to pull it along. Instead, like one of the boats in the harbour, it has a steam engine aboard.

Hydrogen balloon

Wharf

Inn

Stagecoach

Steam carriage

Quay

Some heavy goods are loaded on to barges for transport by canal. Barges can pull a load many times heavier than a horse can on land. A canal basin, where a number of barges can moor along the quay, has recently been built.

Warehouses

Hotel

Lock

Canal basin

Barge

Harbour

Loading cargo

Steamboat

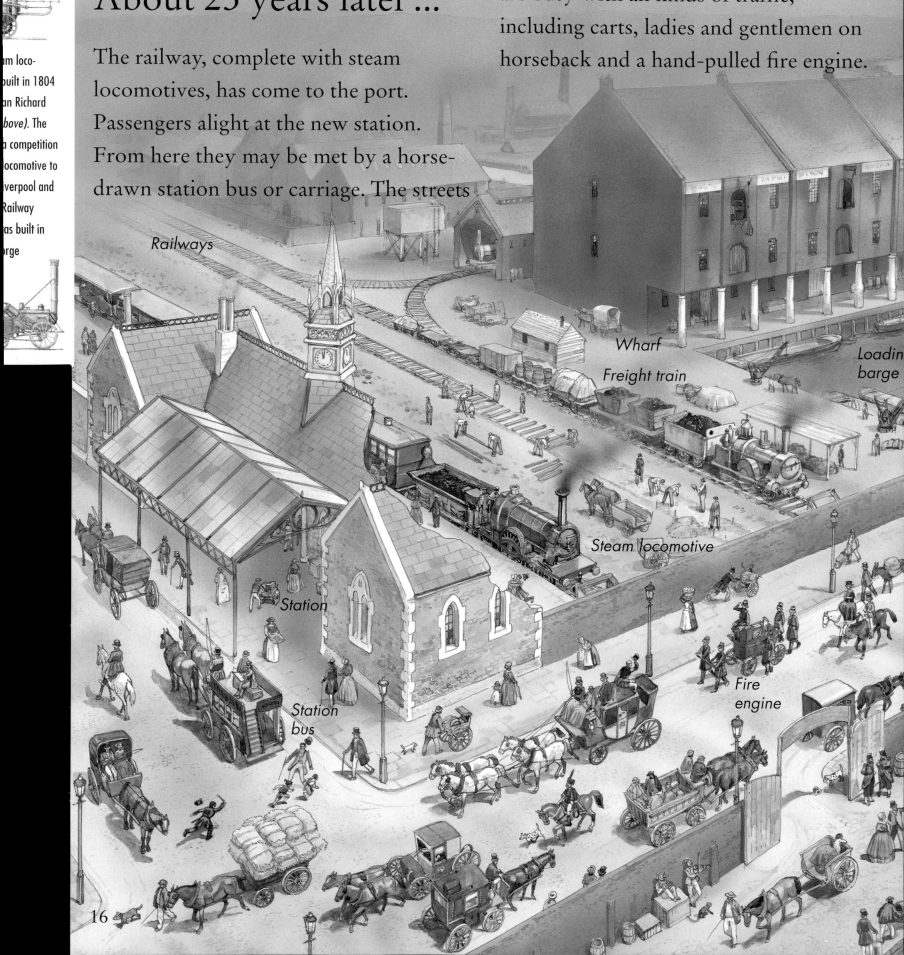

About 25 years later ...

The railway, complete with steam locomotives, has come to the port. Passengers alight at the new station. From here they may be met by a horse-drawn station bus or carriage. The streets including carts, ladies and gentlemen on horseback and a hand-pulled fire engine.

Railways

Wharf

Freight train

Loading barge

Steam locomotive

Station

Station bus

Fire engine

m loco-
uilt in 1804
an Richard
bove). The
competition
ocomotive to
verpool and
Railway
as built in
orge

A paddle-steamer is docked at the quayside. Tomorrow, she will sail for New York across the Atlantic Ocean, a journey that will take just 10 days.

THE FIRST RAILWAYS

Once it had been demonstrated that travel by steam trains was much faster and more comfortable than in horse-drawn vehicles, railways were quickly built all over the world in the 19th century. In America, railways opened up the West for settlement.

Warehouses

Canal basin

Lock gate

Paddle-steamer

Coach

1000 BC

AD 1

1300

1700

1825

1850

17

The age of the car began when German engineer Gottlieb Daimler perfected a small, lightweight petrol-driven engine in the 1880s. The first petrol-driven car was built by Karl Benz in 1885. A three-wheeler, its rear wheels were connected to the engine by belts and a bicycle chain. Benz's wife made the first long journey by car in 1888, a 100-km drive to visit relatives.

About 45 years later ...

The station has been enlarged to handle the increased railway traffic. Goods from nearby factories, cargo ships and the canal are loaded on to freight trains.

A small railway has been built, so people can be carried right up to the steamships that dock at the quay.

There are some important recent inventions to be seen on the busy streets. Among all the various horse-drawn

Factories

Steam locomotive

Station

Quayside railway

Motor car

Motor car

Steam locomotive

Fire engine

Bus

vehicles, steam-powered buses and numerous bicycles (including the Penny Farthing, with its enormous front wheel and tiny rear wheel), are just a few jerky, noisy, petrol-driven motor cars.

SAIL VERSUS STEAM

The first steamships appeared in the early 19th century. Fast sailing ships, known as clippers, still carried most of the ocean trade, but by the 1880s, large steamships, driven by screw propellers, could carry much heavier loads and in all weathers.

1000 BC

AD 1

1300

1700

1825

1850

1895

Castle

Hotel

Barges

Canal basin

Steam tram

Steam-ship

Clipper ship

19

Fifteen years later ...

In just a few years, there have been great changes in the way people travel. On the roads, vehicles with petrol engines are now much more common—although some steam-driven and even horse-drawn vehicles are still in use.

At sea, the days of the ocean liner have arrived. A huge ship, equipped with the latest steam turbine engines and luxury fittings, waits at the quayside.

History was made on 17th December 1903 when US brothers Orville and Wilbur Wright achieved the first controlled flight in an aeroplane *(above)*. It flew for 12 seconds before grounding 37 m away.

One of the first great flights was made by Frenchman Louis Blériot. In 1909, with no means of navigation, he flew his monoplane across the English Channel, crash-landing on the cliffs above Dover. The flight lasted 37 minutes.

Factories

Monoplane

Wharf

Station

Garage

But the newest form of transport is in the skies. A small monoplane flies over the ship's funnels. Meanwhile, a Zeppelin airship, built with a rigid frame filled with bags of hydrogen, cruises by overhead.

Zeppelin airship

Castle

Canal basin

Ocean liner

1000 BC

AD 1

1300

1700

1825

1850

1895

1910

Nearly 30 years later ...

There are now very few horse-drawn vehicles on the roads. Cars and vans fill the busy streets of the city. Lorries unload or pick up goods from the ships moored at the quay. Trams run along rails set into the road. Taxis and coaches wait outside the station for passengers. A petrol station does brisk business.

In 1899, just 14 years after the motor car was invented, *La Jamais Contente* became the first car to exceed 100 km/h.

Using aircraft engines for extra thrust, *Bluebird* took the land speed record at over 400 km/h in the 1930s. Later cars used jet and rocket engines. The current record-holder, *ThrustSSC*, went faster than the speed of sound.

Fighter plane

Canal

Station

Petrol station

Fire engine

New kinds of aircraft fly overhead. A fighter, much faster and more agile than the early monoplane, speeds by. There is also an airliner, designed to carry mail and 20 or 30 passengers over long distances.

Airliner

Castle

Ocean liner

Hotel

Barge

Canal basin

Tram

Destroyer (warship)

Coach

Cargo ship

1000 BC

AD 1

1300

1700

1825

1850

1895

1910

1938

Twenty years later...

Air traffic has grown a great deal since the end of World War II. An airport has been built outside the city and airliners take off and land using its long runway. Some airliners carry 60 to 70 passengers at speeds of 500 kilometres per hour.

Although rocket engines were invented in 1926, space travel began only in the 1950s. The first artificial satellite to be placed into orbit was Sputnik 1 *(above)*. It was launched in October 1957 by a Soviet Vostok rocket *(below)*.

Airport

Airliner taking off

Runway

Aircraft hangar

Dual carriageway

Petrol station

Airliner

Service area

24

Road traffic has also increased and dual carriageway roads have been built. Roundabouts, flyovers, modern petrol stations and service areas also appear.

Trains still run to the port, but most are now diesel or electric powered.

Helicopter

Castle

Canal

Demolished buildings

Canal basin

Diesel train

Station

Harbour

Garage

Docks

1000 BC

AD 1

1300

1700

1825

1850

1895

1910

1938

1958

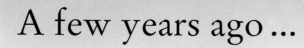

A few years ago ...

A suspension bridge has been built. It carries both road vehicles and high-speed trains. There is also a new airport with larger terminal buildings and a longer runway to cater for supersonic airliners and Jumbo Jets.

Magnetic levitation (maglev) trains are both supported above the tracks and propelled forwards by magnets. They can reach very high speeds because the train does not touch the tracks.

The first vehicle to travel faster than the speed of sound was the rocket-powered aeroplane X-1 *(above)*, called *Glamorous Glennis* by its pilot Chuck Yeager. Since its flight in 1947, other aircraft have flown much faster. The fastest jet was the US Lockheed SR-71 *(below)*, with a top speed of 3911 km/h.

Airport

Jumbo Jet

Concorde (supersonic airliner)

Runway

Motorway

Suspension bridge

High-speed train

A shuttle rail link carries passengers between the city and the airport. Ships in the docks load containers straight from lorries into their holds.

Ferry

Microlight aircraft

Canal basin

Museum of Transport

Shuttle rail link

Harbour

Petrol station

Container port

1000 BC

AD 1

1300

1700

1825

1850

1895

1910

1938

1958

A few years ago

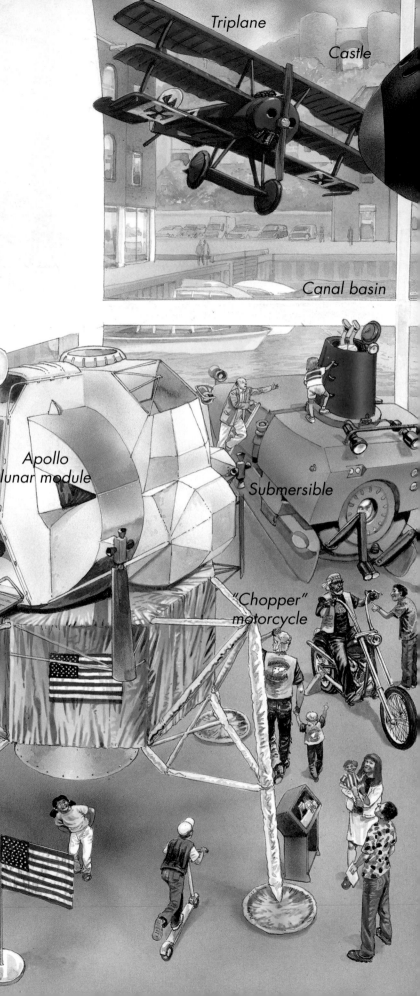

Today

We are inside the city's Museum of Transport. Through its collection of vehicles, it tells the story of transport through the ages, from steam train to Space Shuttle. The museum was built over the site where the remains of a Roman road *(see pages 8-9)* have been discovered. A guide in costume shows the visitors how the road was built.

The Apollo astronauts were launched into space on their way to the Moon in a Saturn V rocket. It went at 10 times the speed of a rifle bullet!

A new form of space transport was designed in the 1970s. The Space Shuttle is the world's first reusable spacecraft. At lift-off, it is attached to a large fuel tank and two boosters. When the fuel is spent, these are cast off. The Shuttle provides a transport link with the scientists aboard the International Space Station.

Triplane

Castle

Canal basin

Model submarine

Apollo lunar module

Submersible

"Chopper" motorcycle

Lunar buggy

28

The visitors have fun gazing at the waxwork models. But you can look back through this book to see some real people in the story of transport ...

Space Shuttle

Steam locomotive (cut away so we can see inside)

Human-powered aircraft

Boucher

Solar-powered car

Penny Farthing

Racing bike

Roman road

Recumbent bicycle

Fire motor-cycle

1000 BC

AD 1

1300

1700

1825

1850

1895

1910

1938

1958

A few years ago

Today

29 ▶

Glossary

Aqueduct A bridge which carries water.

Cargo A ship's freight or load.

Container port A large port where container ships, with their load in sealed containers, load and unload.

Dual carriageway A road with two lanes for traffic in each direction.

Ferry A boat for transporting passengers and vehicles across a stretch of sea or river.

Flyover A long raised section of road allowing one road to cross others without junctions.

Jet A high-speed plane powered by a jet engine. It takes in air at the front and expels hot compressed air from the back of the engine, driving the plane forward.

Lock A device for raising and lowering a boat at the point at which the water level changes on a canal.

Locomotive A railway engine.

Lunar module The part of a spacecraft used in the last stage of the journey to land on the moon.

Microlight A hang glider with an engine-driven propeller attached. It is light and easy to manoeuvre, take off and land in a range of terrains.

Monoplane An aeroplane with a single set of wings.

Orbit The circular or oval-shaped path followed by one object around another. Satellites orbit the Earth.

Paddle steamer A ship powered by a steam engine which turns paddle wheels to move the ship along.

Recumbent bicycle A two-wheeled cycle which the rider pedals from a seated position with legs outstretched, pushing forward on the pedals.

Rocket A vehicle propelled by an engine which creates a stream of hot gases by burning fuel in a chamber.

Satellite A spacecraft that orbits the Earth.

Screw propeller A propeller shaped like a large wood screw which drives a vessel through the water.

Sedan chair A covered chair for a single person carried on two poles.

Stagecoach A passenger coach that runs regularly from one resting place on a journey to the next.

Submarine A vessel that can travel submerged under the water as well as on the surface.

Submersible A miniature submarine, mostly used for research in deep oceans.

Surveyors People who check that land or buildings are suitable for a planned construction or use.

Supersonic Faster than the speed of sound

Suspension bridge A bridge which hangs from steel cables strung between towers.

Triplane An early plane with three sets of wings. Early planes were slow and needed more sets of wings to provide lift.

Index